THE WEATHER MAKERS

The Weather Makers

JOHN FARRIMOND

illustrated by Wendy Hall

As told in Jackanory by
Brigit Forsyth

BRITISH BROADCASTING CORPORATION

By the same author:

THE HILLS OF HEAVEN

Published by the
British Broadcasting Corporation,
35 Marylebone High Street, London W1M 4AA

ISBN 0 563 17738 1
First published 1980

Printed and bound in Great Britain
by W & J Mackay Limited, Chatham

To Barbara, Edith and Jean,
who taught me a lot at Park High School

I

They were halfway up Rimington Pike when Tommy flopped down, staring upwards into the thick fog.

"Have a minute, lass!"

Jenn turned her head, the brightness of her eyes visible even through the grey murk.

"Your legs gone a'ready, Tommy?" she jeered at him good-naturedly. "You, what were gonna nip up Rimington Pike in one go!"

"Nothin' to do wi' me legs," Tommy cried, grinning as she slithered on the rough, stony path before dropping down beside him.

"It's freezin' on this stone, Tommy!" Jenn cried, jumping up almost at once.

"On'y to them what's soft!"

"Five minutes sittin' on that stone, an' you'll be hard, lad. Frozen hard to it!"

"I've been thinkin'," Tommy mused, peering upwards into the fog which had been covering the town, and the Pike since early morning. "Somethin' I heard on t'wireless this mornin'. Freezin' fog."

"You can't hear fog!" Jenn laughed at him in deep sarcasm.

"Don't try to be smart, lass, I'm serious."

"Go on then!"

"Lass, you're right about this stone!" Tommy jumped up quickly, stamping his feet on the steel-hard, frozen ground. "What time is it, you reckon?"

"Can't see t'church clock from up here!"

"Come out o' t'knife drawer this mornin', ain't you? Never heard anybody as sharp!"

"What about this freezin' fog?" Jenn demanded impatiently. "Nine hundred feet to t'top, remember, more maybe. An' us on'y halfway yet, I bet. Fog'll have gone before we get up there, then it'll be a wasted trip." She studied him a moment, puckering her lips. "Reckon it's a wasted trip now, I do that!"

"There you go!"

"We-ll," Jenn persisted, rubbing her hands together with a shiver. "Sounds to sense, how c'n anybody get to t'top o' fog? I don't believe there is a top to fog; when it comes it covers all the world, an' all the sky. Right up to heaven."

"There you go wi' your stupid girl talk!" Tommy cried. "You know nothin', an' not much o' that, neither. Come on, in another ten minutes I'll show you I'm right. I've seen clouds close to t'top o' this hill, an' so have you, many a time. I once knew a lad what were up there when a cloud came over. Went right through him, he swears it, an' him wet through

after it had gone!"

"Steam from some factory chimney." Jenn laughed that off. "There's lots o' 'em in Arpull. Factory chimneys is what causes fog, I learnt that at school."

Tommy pulled at her coat in sudden impatience. "Come on, lass! We all know what *causes* fog, nobody ever found out if there's a roof to it. You an' me'll be the first. We could get our names in them books o' records. First people to see the roof o' a fog!"

"Roof o' a fog!" Jenn laughed in his face. "For a lad o' eleven you talk daft!"

"For a lass o' ten you act stupid!"

Jenn shot out her tongue at him, and, honour satisfied, they moved upwards into the fog. Neither of them had ever seen fog as thick as this; it seemed to merge into the hill itself.

It was a Saturday morning in mid-December, and it suddenly struck Jenn that they could have been at the local cinema. They could have been warm and snug, lost in some space film, not groping around the Pike in dense fog. "Daft!" she cried, after some minutes had passed. "We're daft! Suppose we can't find our road back, eh?"

"Keep goin'," Tommy urged her urgently. "Can't be much further to t'top, we've been climbin' for ages."

"Tommy!" Jenn cried suddenly. "What's that?"

"Can't see anythin'."

"There *is* somethin' – a shape. Right up in t'fog!"

Jenn grabbed at Tommy's coat in sudden fright.

"It's t' fog, it makes shapes sometimes! Come on!"

"It *was* somethin' I tell you!"

Suddenly there was a kind of a howling sound, and the rattle of loosened stones on the path. Tommy felt Jenn's fingers pressing tightly into his wrist.

"Wolves!" Jenn cried. "There's wolves after us!"

"Wolves my aunt Fanny!" Tommy jeered, but the howling came at them again, and he stiffened. "Ain't no *wolves* on Rimington Pike!"

"Some wild dog then! Let's go back, Tommy, please!"

"On'y another few minutes, lass! We can't give up now."

Suddenly a long black shape appeared, and then another. Right above them in the fog. The howling came again. They just stood there, too utterly scared to move.

The black shapes circled round, moved in behind, still howling. When they came nearer it was suddenly obvious to both Tommy and Jenn what they were. Wolves! Wild, vicious howling wolves, running loose on the side of a Lancashire hill!

"Come on!" Tommy cried, grabbing Jenn's hand in his. "We'll rush 'em, we've gotta rush 'em if we want to get back home!"

"They'll attack us if we do!"

"They're closin' in, lass! We gotta rush 'em!"

"Oh, Tommy!"

As they stood there, still rooted to the ground, the

wolves moved towards them. Tommy and Jenn stepped back up the path instinctively.

The wolves moved in again, and again Tommy and Jenn retreated upwards, towards the summit.

They were stumbling backwards, falling over

stones, and deep holes, their hands clasped tight together.

Suddenly Tommy decided on flight. "We gotta run, lass!" he cried, letting go of Jenn's hand. "On our own!"

"Don't leave me, Tommy!" Jenn cried. "Don't leave me on my own!"

"I'll not leave you, but we gotta run separate, to t'tower. If we c'n jus' get to t'tower, an' climb in we'll be safe!"

Jenn began to run beside him as Tommy started out for the summit. The wolves followed, keeping their distance, but the howling they made seemed somehow to be all around.

Up, and up, and up. Through the thick fog, stumbling often, and their breath coming hard.

"Tommy! I – I can't – go any more," Jenn panted.

Tommy pulled at her hand as the black shapes moved in on them. "You've gotta keep goin', lass! Keep goin'!"

"I can't," Jenn whispered hoarsely, and she sank down to the cold hard ground.

"They'll get us!" Tommy cried breathlessly, trying to pull her to her feet.

He peered down at the shapes, and all round. There were animals looming out of the fog everywhere – except above them. As if – as if they were leaving a way of escape.

Jenn stumbled to her feet, her face full of her distress.

"Come on, lass!" Tommy urged her. "We'll be OK. I know it! I don't think – these wolves're – real!"

"They're real!" Jenn almost sobbed. She started off again towards the summit, vanishing suddenly in the fog.

"Jenn!" Tommy shouted after her in alarm. "Jenn!"

There was no answer. Nothing except the howling of the wolves. There was nowhere to look except into the blanket of fog, and even this was solid to his frightened eyes. A wall almost, surrounding him, making a prisoner of him, with the menacing shapes outside.

"Jenn! Jenn!" He started to climb the hill that was the last obstacle before the tower itself, shouting her name in a voice which became ever shriller. As he moved upwards the fog pulled away, as if reluctant to let him through, then closed ever tighter in on him.

The howling had ceased, there was no sign of the wolves. Just him, alone in all the world, but a small world indeed. Pressing in, enveloping his body.

"Jenn!" Tommy stopped climbing. He was no

longer able to see even the ground at his feet. "Jenn!"

There was no answer.

He began to move upwards, calling her name at intervals. The fog seemed now to tug at him, and finally he had to physically force himself through it. Then the pressure was gone, the fog vanished.

"Tommy, where've you been?" It was Jenn's voice, right above him! He looked upwards, and there she was, her thin face full of wonder. Tommy just stood there, staring at her. There was no fear in Jenn's eyes now, nothing but this look of sheer wonder.

"Where've I been!" Tommy was aware only dimly of his lips framing the words. "Lookin' for you, lass, what else? You jus' vanished into t'fog, an' you never answered when I shouted! What're you lookin' at, anyway?"

"Magic, Tommy, magic," Jenn whispered. "You were so right – when you said there was a roof to this fog. I – I pushed through it – like – like a turnstile. Then it was *gone*, don't you see? Jus' look at that sky."

Tommy looked. Above him stood the old tower which had been on top of Rimington for hundreds of years, a famous landmark all across Lancashire. Now it seemed that the tower, and the final hill on which it stood, hung motionless in a sea of fog. Above was an orange sky, and a sun that shone like a newly-polished brass ball.

"Never seen anythin' like this in all my life," Jenn whispered.

Tommy nodded, too overcome to find words to describe this magic. He began to walk slowly along the bottom of this final hill beneath the tower, shaking his head endlessly. At his feet was the fog, except that it didn't seem merely fog any more, but truly a sea, an ocean. He let his eyes feast on the great expanse of it; it went out of sight into the distance. It must cover all the world, white, cold, yet strangely inviting.

"Wish I'd a camera, I do that, lass!" he cried, spinning round on Jenn, now close behind him. "Nobody'll believe what we saw, when we go back, nobody'll believe us!"

"It don't matter, Tommy," Jenn whispered. "We've seen it."

"Aye, we've seen it, lass. Bet we could sail a boat on that sea – if we'd a boat!"

"Where to?" Jenn cried.

"Next hill, wherever that might be. We could – we could anchor off it, explore it like it was some desert island!"

"A desert island in the middle o' Lancashire!"

"Ain't no hills as high as Rimington, anyway," Tommy grinned. "On'y Blackpool Tower. Aye, Blackpool Tower, lass, we could get to t'top o' it for nowt. Might even hire out the boat. 'Any more for sailin'; top o' Blackpool Tower to t'top o' Rimington, forty P!' "

Tommy looked down at the fog, puzzled.

"What's do, Tommy?" Jenn asked.

He didn't answer, but went down quickly on his haunches, leaning forward as if to scoop a handful.

"Thick enough to stuff pillows wi'," Jenn laughed. "You takin' some home then?"

"Thick enough to – to skate on!" Tommy cried, exultantly. He looked at her in new wonder. "Didn't I tell you, lass, about there bein' 'freezin'' fog? Well, it's *froze!*"

Jenn laughed down into his face. "Froze! How c'n fog freeze?"

"Feel at it then!"

"You're havin' me on!"

"Try it wi' your clog. Go on! T'fog's froze, I tell you!"

Jenn laughed uncertainly, then put her foot down hesitantly into what she was certain was merely thick fog. The clog hit a solid barrier, and she pulled her foot away as if she'd been burned.

"Well?" Tommy cried excitedly, as she knelt beside him.

"Solid!" Jenn whispered in awe. "*Solid fog!*"

"Freezin' fog, lass, like it said on t'wireless."

Jenn looked at the "fog", then at Tommy, and shook her head.

"We're dreamin', it's a – a trick! Tommy, I'm scared."

"Nowt to be scared about, lass. Jus' imagine, we've seen somethin' nobody else ever see! Solid fog – an' a sky what looks like no other sky ever did. Except in – in picture books maybe."

Jenn stared a long while at the sky of deep orange, and the shiny brass sun. "Aye, Tommy, you're right," she whispered. "Like – a picture book."

They knelt at the edge of the fog, staring now at each other.

"Not like Rimington Pike, not any more," Jenn said slowly.

"Tower's still yonder," Tommy put in, nodding upwards.

"Aye."

"Somethin' funny goin' on, there is that," Tommy mused.

"I'm scared," Jenn said suddenly jumping to her feet. "Let's go back down!"

"What about them howlin' wolves?"

"You think maybe we – imagined 'em, Tommy?" Jenn asked him earnestly. "You said they weren't real, remember?"

"Some feelin' I had. Come to me we were runnin' from shadows."

"That howlin' was real enough, it was that! Never been as scared in me life!"

"You really want to go back down, lass?"

"Aye."

"You wouldn't like to – er – explore this fog?"

"You mean – *walk* on it?"

"Why not? I bet it's a yard thick, safe as houses."

"You're not gettin' me walkin' on t'top o' fog! Might seem solid now, but suppose it went back to bein' normal while we were skatin' across it? We'd land wi' a bang on some factory roof in Arpull! Maybe six hundred feet straight down!"

Tommy sighed, looking across the sea of fog, ice, or whatever it was surrounding them. "OK lass, OK," he said in resignation. He grinned then. "If we did fall on some factory roof, lass, from six hundred feet, we'd look like two pancakes. Folk would never know we fell off t'top o' fog. We'll go back, an' tell 'em ourselves what we see."

"Who'll believe a tale like this?" Jenn laughed, happy that Tommy had agreed to go back down the hill. What had happened had been like acting a part in some fairy story. There'd be no happy ending till they got back home.

"Ready, lass?" Tommy asked, searching round for the spot they'd come up through the fog. They walked along the bottom of the hill on which the tower stood, looking for any sign of a break in the barrier. After some hundred yards Tommy stopped, scratching his head. "I'm sure we've passed it!"

"Tommy," Jenn cried in a suddenly very frightened voice.

"What?"

"We're trapped up here! There's no way down! Can't you see? Fog's gone solid, all around this hill!"

Tommy looked round at her, looked down at the fog. He stamped his foot, and the sound echoed, and re-echoed across the great sea of it, like the cracking of a thousand windows.

"I never thought o' that, lass. No way down!"

"What'll we *do*?"

"Wait till it melts, lass, what else?"

"Might take days!"

"We might smash it, I'll find some big stone to smash a way through!"

They both scouted round the bottom of the hill, and Tommy picked up a stone at last. He tried to break the ice, but it was impossible to even hold the stone properly.

"Oh, Tommy, we'll freeze to death before they find us!"

"We'll be all right, lass, you see."

"No food, nothin' to drink. They'll find us frozen stiff; nobody will ever know what we see!"

"Scout round t'bottom o' this hill, lass!" Tommy urged her. "Bound to be some way down."

"You an' your frozen fog!" Jenn cried in sudden anger. "I was daft for takin' you on, comin' up here in weather like this!"

"Come on!" Tommy said.

They hurried along the edge of the frozen fog, right round the hill. There was no escape, nothing – just the tower above them, and the ocean of fog in all directions at their feet.

"No use, lass!" Tommy cried, his breath coming out of his lips like a series of miniature fogs. "We're trapped all right."

"What are we goin' to do?"

"Let's go up to the tower. On'y place up here what looks – well human."

"Nowt up there, jus' a lot o' stones!"

"Maybe we'd best climb in there for some sort o' shelter. If we don't find a way down soon."

"No roof on t'tower, anybody knows that!"

"Let's go, anyway," Tommy gave her a quick grin. "You were so sure there weren't a roof on that blinkin' fog, remember?"

They trudged up the last steep hill, and reached the side of the old tower. They'd been up to it a hundred times over the years. It was a curious square tower made of heavy stones. The windows had been boarded up long ago, although since then vandals had broken them again. It was difficult to climb up but Tommy managed it and was about to look in.

"See anythin'?" Jenn shouted up.

"Wait a minute!" Tommy spluttered down at her. Then the air was rent with the howling of wolves, Tommy dropped down in a flurry. "Run, lass, run!" he cried, grabbing her hand.

Jenn allowed him to lead her, her hand outstretched to the full to keep up with him. She dared to look back, to see the wolves tearing down the hill after them. More than once Tommy tumbled headlong, and Jenn on top of him.

They reached the bottom of the hill, and were stopped in their tracks by the sea of fog.

The howling was deafening now, and around them

in a half circle, stood the wolves.

"Tommy, they'll kill us! They'll kill us!" Jenn sobbed.

"We gotta go on the ice!" Tommy cried.

"They'll follow us!"

"We'll have to chance it. Come on, lass, we gotta risk it!"

Jenn stood there in sheer fright, torn between her fear of the animals, and her fear of the unknown. Suddenly the wolves seemed to move inwards, reducing the circle. Their howling increased in volume, and she could see the wet redness of their mouths.

"Run then, Tommy, run!" Jenn cried.

Without a testing foot, or a moment of hesitation, they ran hand in hand out on to the roof of the fog.

2

"Tommy, wait for me!"

Tommy stopped running, skidding on the ice. He turned, and saw Jenn floundering along nervously, fearfully, her feet slipping about. The wolves were still howling, but for a minute they just paced about at the edge of the ice. Tommy went back, and took Jenn's hand in his, and they stood there a moment looking back fearfully.

"Come on, Tommy, please!" Jenn cried, tugging at his hand. "We've got to get away from them, they'll be on the ice in a minute!"

"No they won't!" a voice whirred behind them. "Not till I give them permission." A kind of crispy, rustling voice.

The two children whirled round in complete surprise.

"Who——" Tommy started to say, then he just gaped.

There was nobody there, at least, nobody human. Just a large, man-sized book. Cut out in the

unmistakable shape of a woman! An enormous copy of cut-out books Jenn had handled in the local bookshop.

Jenn stared at the book, hovering there on its end, her eyes glassy with wonder.

"I'm sure I heard a voice, Tommy!"

"Never mind a voice, where on earth did *that* come from?" Tommy spluttered.

"How do I know?" Jenn shot back at him irritably. "Books don't talk, anyway."

"This one does!" The book rustled at them angrily.

"It *is* the book talkin'!" Tommy cried.

"That's silly!" Jenn said firmly. "How c'n you talk wi'out a mouth?"

"Does the wind have a mouth?" the book whirred at them. "It mutters, and moans, and screams sometimes."

"She's right, lass," Tommy nodded, still gaping at the book.

"You're as silly as she is!" Jenn jeered. All this being chased by wolves, and walking on the top of fog against her will indeed! Now a book which said it could talk!

"Silly, am I?" the book flicked a dozen or so pages angrily. "Not as silly as you two *humans*, stuck on the wrong side!"

"The wrong side o' what?" Tommy asked her curiously.

"This of course!" the book seemed to stamp the

bottom of her hardback covers like feet on the ice. "The barrier. You must have got through just before the fog set."

"Like a jelly, you mean?" Jenn asked. "Did you pour it out of some big pan, ready to serve with custard?"

"A lot of cheek you have, for a small girl," the book whirred.

"I'm ten," Jenn said proudly.

"You like being ten?"

"I'd rather be eleven, or sixteen."

"I'm afraid you won't ever be more than ten."

"Why ever not?"

"Because nothing ever grows older up here. Not even humans, I should imagine. Ten you are, ten you'll always be."

"We're not stoppin' up here!" Tommy cried angrily. "I want to play football for Manchester United! I can't if I'm on'y a kid all my life!" He walked over to the book, swaggering a bit to show that he wasn't afraid. "Who are you, anyway, to say things like that?"

"I'm the Weather."

"The *weather?*" Tommy said, puzzled.

"With a capital W."

"The weather, with a capital W!" Jenn laughed. "How c'n anybody *be* the weather?"

A bird went flying past, just beyond Tommy. He stared after it, watched it intently till it vanished across the ice. Then he spun on Jenn. "See that bird,

lass? It – it's got writin' on it!"

"Don't be stupid, Tommy."

"I saw it, plain enough! Writin' on it, an' – an' it looked like it'd been cut from a book!"

"Clever boy!" the book whirred. "I'll make something of you, see if I don't. Are you clever too, girl?"

"Cleverer than him," Jenn said with satisfaction. "Ten places up on him in class."

"I had flu, didn't I?" Tommy defended himself.

"A bird wi' writin' on!" Jenn sneered. "You'll be seein' pink elephants in a bit, Tommy!"

"More than likely," the book whirred.

They stared at her in fresh surprise. "You mean," Jenn asked, "that there really *are* pink elephants up here?"

"Not if I can help it!"

"But you jus' said—" Tommy challenged her.

"Never mind that, boy!" the book cut at him, crisp as the flick of new pound notes. "You don't know anything, do you! About what goes on up here!"

"Never knew anythin' went on up here!" Jenn said crossly. "We're dreamin' all this, Tommy, dreamin' it!"

"Before you're much older you'll have nightmares I shouldn't wonder," the book snapped at her. "A hard life up here, for everybody. No slackers here. First sign of that, and I banish them to the Wind Tunnels."

"The Wind Tunnels?" Tommy said, gaping at the book.

"Oh, phizz!" the book crackled impatiently. "All this talk, and nothing *said!* I'll explain. You make books, don't you? On the other side of the Barrier?"

"There you go again, with this – Barrier!" Jenn said.

"Shut up till I tell you to speak. This second."

"If I don't, what then?" Jenn retorted.

"I'll set the wolves on you."

Both Jenn and Tommy spun round in alarm. The wolves were still at the edge of the ice. The book flicked her pages briefly, and the whole pack moved

in, scurrying forward eagerly, hungrily.

"Oh, no!" Jenn cried in sudden terror. "Don't let them any closer, please!"

"Say you're sorry then!" snapped the book.

"I'm sorry," said Jenn meekly.

The book seemed to preen its pages with deep satisfaction, then flicked a page at the advancing wolves. They turned, squealing, and ran; back off the ice, and up the steep hill towards the tower.

"It's magic!" Tommy cried. "Magic!"

"There's no such thing as magic, boy!" the book cut her pages in two sections, then slammed them together on each word. It was the most impressive form of italics Tommy had ever seen.

Jenn, however, was still clinging to her black mood. "There's no such thing as a talking book which says it's the weather, with a capital W, either!"

"You are a tiresome child, aren't you?" the book whirred. "I'll be looking forward to experimenting on you!"

"Experimentin' on me?" Jenn cried in alarm.

"Why not? You seem quite resigned to seeing wolves, and birds cut from books, don't you?"

"You mean," Tommy cried, "that bird I saw was really cut out of some book?"

"Of course. The Never-never bird."

"I never heard o' one o' *them!*" Tommy said, laughing at the name.

"You mean," Jenn put in, "that – *everythin'* up here, them wolves, birds, an' even you, was cut from some book?"

"Not me, silly girl! I'm the Weather. Look!" She flicked her pages from front to back, then all the way to the covers again. "Three hundred and sixty-five pages. One for each day of the year. It's time someone knew about the trouble I have, every day of every year! Look here for instance; January – – – " The book leaned forward, flicking back a few pages. "Six storms, two bouts of hailstones, and seven freeze-ups to get out. Not to mention an assortment of fogs, and drizzles! And what happens? No supplies to speak of!"

"You really mean that you are the Weather?" Jenn asked her.

"Who else? Did you think weather just happened then?"

"Course it does!" Tommy scoffed. "Any kid knows that!"

"Does he now!" The book was positively flashing her pages back and forth in her anger. "What about clouds then?"

"They go where the wind blows 'em," Tommy said confidently.

"And who fixes which way the wind blows?"

"Nobody fixes t'wind!" Jenn put in, laughing.

"Phizz! You think that, do you? *I* fix the weather because I am the Weather. With a capital W! There are only so many storm clouds in all the world, you know that surely?"

"I never counted 'em." Tommy laughed.

"No, nobody counts them, but they expect them to come along on time like – like buses, or trains! I'm the one who has to fix up this yearly timetable for clouds, you know. Storm clouds, puffs, fluffs, woollies. I need clouds for rain, don't I?"

"All we need is a cricket match, or a carnival!" Tommy said in deep sarcasm. "So *you're* the one who causes all the trouble!"

"Trouble? Phizz! You don't know what trouble is, my boy, but you will, you will. My wolves did a fine job driving you up here before the fog set solid; I must reward them for their cunning."

"You mean," Jenn cried in amazement, "that they actually did that? Drove us up here?"

"I felt it, lass, felt it!" Tommy cut in. "They herded us up through the top o' the fog. Like we were blinkin' sheep!"

"Correct," the Weather whirred with new satisfaction. "Like sheep, but humans indeed. Two pairs of hands to help me through my yearly task! For ever!"

"You'll be lucky!" Tommy cried in sudden anger. "I'm off home, I've a football match on this afternoon. I'm not stoppin' up here for *ever!*"

"Nobody plays football today, boy, anywhere from the Midlands to the Scottish border. Thick fog will last all day, and half the night. I fixed that up weeks ago."

"You'd no right! I was go'nna score a hat-trick today!"

An animal went past between them, and Jenn cried out: "Look, Tommy, a cut-out rabbit! So there truly are animals up here, cut from picture books!"

"It was a cat!" Tommy said firmly. "I c'n tell t'difference between a rabbit, an' a cat. Even if it is cut from a book!"

The Weather made her pages whirr and rustle loudly, in what seemed to be jeering laughter.

"It's a cat on one side, a rabbit on the other! Your people's silly fault for printing pictures in magazines on opposite sides of the page. When we cut out one animal we have to cut out the other. Poor dears don't know what they are, or which way they're coming and going!"

"That's cruel!" Jenn cried.

"What can I do, girl? I need every animal I can get. Don't you see? All this *work*, and only animals, and birds to do it. You've heard of 'bird-brain', and 'stupid as a donkey'? It's true, you know, true."

"If you can make such magic with animals, and things," Jenn said shrewdly, "why don't you cut out people instead? Come to that, where do you get all your picture books up here on the Pike?"

"They blow up, of course! I fix magazine day on

the first of every month. Remember, I control the wind. Magazines come out every month. So I do a few whirlwinds along the High Street, and we gather the harvest of books."

"Where do you stack 'em?" Tommy asked, his curiosity taking over once more.

"In the tower, of course."

"Don't talk to me about the tower!" Tommy cried. "When I tried to climb up there them wolves o' yours nearly got me!"

"Serves you right. Don't you ever go near that tower again, not if you value your life!"

"Why not?"

"Never mind. Wolves aren't the only animals, and *things* in the tower. Don't you ever go near again, I need your two pairs of hands."

"For ever?" Tommy asked her, watching the book intently.

"For ever."

"Right, lass!" Tommy cried, grabbing Jenn's hand. "We're off!"

"Where, Tommy, where? There's no way down, we tried, an' – an' *she* says there isn't any way down through that barrier!"

"Flee if you wish, flee!" the Weather snapped at them sharply. "Run your silly legs off, but please don't harm your hands. Hands I need, desperately."

"You won't get ours!" Tommy cried bravely. "We're off!"

"Where will you go?"

"We'll find somewhere, there's gotta be *somewhere!*"

"Blackpool's nice, even in winter," the Weather whirred. "Or Southport. Eighteen miles or so, as the crow flies. A pity you can't. I must warn you though, mind you don't fall through the vents on the way!"

"Vents?" Tommy said, quite puzzled.

"All those factory chimneys belching smoke, you know. By some chemical magic the smoke forces a way past the barrier. It puffs through, a thick, black fog, hovering for *miles*. Fog over fog you might say. You'd be down one of the vents, and hurtling hundreds of feet before you'd started coughing out the thick smoke. Go if you must. I'll be here when you come back. *If* you come back."

Jenn felt near to tears by now, but she wouldn't let Tommy see her distress. "Why don't you cut *people* from books?" she cried. "Use them instead of keeping us here for ever?"

"My dear child, I'd *love* to use people, but do you know? It won't work with people! Only animals, and birds, and – things."

"Things?" Jenn asked her, her eyes popping now.

"Things. Like the ones in the tower."

"Perhaps," Jenn persisted, "you didn't try hard enough. I'm sure picture book people are really no different from picture book animals!" She wasn't a bit keen to dwell on what the "things" in the Tower might be. Certainly she'd never, *ever* go to find out!

"People are very awkward. I've always found them so," the Weather flipped her pages crossly. "No matter, *if* you come back I'll experiment on you, it might work, it just might work!"

"You won't touch her!" Tommy cried, shaping up to the Weather with his fists up.

"Don't try anything with me, boy!" the Weather cut at him like the cracking of whips. "I'll have my wolves on you! Go, if you must, before I lose my temper!"

"Come on, lass," said Tommy. "Let's go."

"What about the vents?" Jenn asked fearfully.

"We'll be careful."

"What about the smoke?"

"We'll put our hankies over our mouth."

"I've lost mine."

"You would. Come on, lass, we gotta try somethin'!"

They started to half walk, half skate, across the ice. After a few yards they could hear the Weather laughing. The great gusts of mocking laughter reminded Tommy of huge waves crashing on the shore at Blackpool.

The sound put fear into him, but he didn't want Jenn to know, she was frightened enough as it was. "Come on, lass, we'll find some way out. I've an idea o' one place at least we might get down to earth again."

"Where, Tommy, where?" Jenn cried.

"Blackpool Tower, lass! It's a heck o' a way, but if we c'n make it past them vents we c'n go down the steps there, or – or even in t'lift!"

"What about t'Barrier, Tommy? *If* we get there, *if!*"

"We'll get there, lass, never fear. There's one thing favourin' us. This is *ice*, remember. We'll skate! We're both wearin' clogs."

"Aye, clogs!" Jenn cried peevishly. "I hate clogs! They're years out o' fashion. Me mam said I had to have 'em, because she always wore clogs, an' me dad's a clog an' shoe repairer. I bet I'm the on'y lass in Arpull what wears *clogs!*"

"Thank your lucky stars, lass, that you do," Tommy told her. "Remember how I taught you to skate wi' 'em last winter, remember?"

"I remember, hurt me ankles somethin' shockin'."

"Forget your ankles! Come on, skate, lass, skate!"

Jenn looked at him, then turned her eyes back towards where the Weather still hovered. Her loud laughter still echoed across the ice.

"Right, Tommy!" Jenn cried, spinning back on him. "Right! Blackpool Tower, here we come!"

3

They started to skate across the ice, slowly at first because Jenn was really out of practice, then faster as she remembered the knack. In her concentration she forgot her fear of what might lie ahead. She hated her clogs all right, and always looked forward to Sundays when she was allowed to wear her best shoes.

Skating with clogs had long been common practice around Lancashire. It was hard on the ankles till you finally got the knack, and this knack was like learning to ride a bike. Difficult at first, then suddenly easy as the idea clicked in your mind. Jenn had leaned her ankles over, and inward, starting to press against the ice. The inside "iron" on each clog became suddenly the blade of the skate, cutting firmly into the ice.

After some minutes they were really going, swish-swish. Across the roof of Lancashire, on towards Blackpool Tower.

They stopped now and then, for a breather, and once, Jenn, her face flushed with excitement, looked across at a breathless Tommy, grinning. "I'll beat you to Blackpool, Tommy!"

Tommy laughed. "We'll see, lass, we'll see. You still scared?"

"Course I'm scared! Who wouldn't be?"

Tommy looked round. There was nothing except ice in all directions, nothing except the strange, orange sky, and the brass ball sun. No smoke, anywhere.

"I think that Weather was havin' us on, lass, about them vents," Tommy said. "Not a wisp o' smoke anywhere, right as far as we c'n see."

"She's sly, that one," agreed Jenn. Then she put her hand to her forehead, staring ahead. "Can't see no Blackpool Tower yet. I'll bet we've gone *miles*."

"We've gone some way, I bet at that," Tommy nodded, following her example. Then he gave her a shove. "We'll not see Blackpool Tower, stupid! Not like if we come on it while walkin' along t'Prom! Wi' all this ice-fog frozen into it high up we'll be lucky to see t'tip! If I remember there's some lights shinin' on top o' Blackpool Tower – warning for aircraft. We look for them, an' wi' luck we'll find 'em."

"Then all we gotta do is to skate off in that direction till we reach it," Jenn said excitedly.

"We'll reach it, lass," Tommy assured her. "Then our troubles will be over. Come on lass, skate!"

After some minutes at top speed, Tommy pulled to a halt. "Watch what you're doin', stupid!" Jenn cried. "I could have mown you down. Stoppin' sudden like that!"

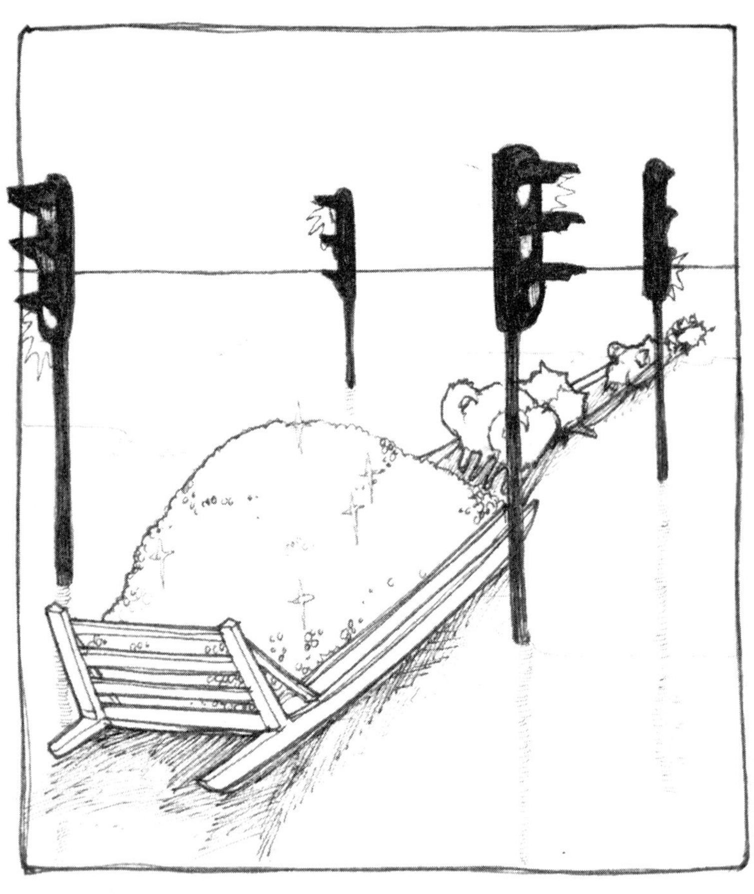

"Red light," Tommy told her matter-of-factly. "Can't go through a crossin' wi' t'lights against us."

Jenn gaped at him, then her eyes almost turned into glass marbles as she realised he wasn't joking. There really were traffic lights just ahead, with a red light facing them, and the reflections of green on the ice at right angles. "Tommy, what . . ." Jenn began,

but Tommy shut her up sharply. "Hush, somethin' comin'!"

As he spoke a team of huskies came across the lights from south to north. They were pulling hard at some large vehicle piled high with a gleaming cargo, bright in the light of the copper sun. The vehicle seemed to glide along smoothly on runners. It went off into the mist as a voice shouted "Mush! Mush!" from the top of the load. Yet there seemed to be nobody up there . . .

"Tommy," Jenn whispered urgently, "what is it?"

"A low loader," Tommy replied, still staring at the procession.

"What the heck is a low loader?"

"You've seen 'em, lass. Down in Arpull. Long, low things, what carry tractors; only this one's carryin' somethin' else."

"What?" Jenn persisted.

"How do I know?"

"Some more comin'!" Jenn cried, as another load came by behind a fresh team of huskies.

As Tommy and Jenn watched expectantly other teams followed at fixed intervals, each tugging hard to keep the load behind it moving. It was some time before the lights changed to amber, then green. They crossed over, skating steadily over the ice till they had cleared the traffic lights. There, both turned as one, staring back at the way the convoy had gone. The last one was just visible in the mist.

"What you reckon them were, Tommy?" Jenn demanded.

"Let's nip after 'em, an' find out!"

Tommy skated off into the distance towards where the last low loader was. Jenn caught up with him, eager, curious. They grabbed a handful of the load, staring at what they'd got.

"Marbles!" Jenn cried. "Cold as ice!"

Tommy laughed in her face. "Marbles me foot! Hailstones, that's what they are. Loads an' loads o' hailstones!"

"Daft, all this!" Jenn cried in near hysteria. "Traffic lights on top o' frozen fog! Convoys o' hailstones bein' delivered to drop on people. They hurt, hailstones! I've seen babies cry out through hailstones: an' dogs, an' cats scutterin' away in fright."

"Aye, like stones sometimes, hailstones. A pity we can't . . ."

"Can't what, Tommy?"

"Re-route them low loaders. Where they won't hurt folk walkin' about their business."

"Oh, Tommy, if on'y we could!"

"We'll do it lass, come on! After that first low loader!"

"What if the driver attacks us?"

"We'll have to chance that. Come on!"

They sped along, skirting the first four loads with their tugging, eager team of huskies. They reached the first load, skating now beside the leading pair of huskies. Close up the dogs seemed huge, yet somehow gentle.

"What c'n we do to stop 'em?" Jenn cried, looking at Tommy.

"We'll be the leaders, lass! You an' me. Take a hold o' that leading husky. I'll take the other. We'll guide them away from that witch what calls herself the Weather."

Jenn looked back at the huge sled, fearfully. "The driver, Tommy! He'll maybe attack us!"

"You're not scared o' a parrot, are you?"

"A parrot! You mean – "

"Who do you reckon is makin' wi' all that 'Mush!' Ain't any folk up here except us two."

Tommy jammed his hand into the harness of his lead husky. "Mush!" he shouted at the top of his voice. "Mush!"

"Mush!" Jenn cried. "Mush!"

They started to move on the ice, and the convoy kept going steadily forward in the mist. Mile after mile it seemed. Jenn was about to call to Tommy when he stopped the convoy himself, pulling his husky to a halt.

"Whoa there! Whoa!"

"What's do, Tommy?" Jenn asked.

"A vent, lass, see?" pointed Tommy as he approached the gaping hole. Straight ahead, there was smoke curling up from a huge hole in the ice. They both left the huskies, each one with print on one side, clearly cut from some picture book by the Weather.

"That Weather was right then, about t'danger along here," Jenn whispered.

"If you'd not seen that hole in time we'd have fallen down into it."

They moved over the very edge of the vent. There was smoke coming up slowly, and it felt warm, leaning over the side.

Tommy could even make out how thick the ice was, at least two yards. Below that was just a haze of smoke.

"Factory chimney, lass," Tommy murmured in awe. "Must be scores on 'em around. We'll have to be careful, all right."

One of the huskies started to howl, and they both jumped to their feet in alarm as the other dogs took up the chorus.

"What is it Tommy?" Jenn cried, staring all round.

"Don't know, lass. Unless . . ."

"Unless what?"

"That Weather! She's signallin' to 'em, I bet! Tellin' 'em to get a move on wi' these hailstones!"

"Mush!" the leading parrot called. "Mush!"

"Whoa!" Tommy shouted, running back to grab at the leading husky as it started to dig its feet into the ice. "Whoa!"

"Mush!" the parrot called.

Jenn grabbed at the other side of the leader, and stared at Tommy for guidance. "What are we goin' to do? They'll be off wi' all these hailstones in a minute!"

"Unhitch 'em!" Tommy cried urgently.

"What?"

"Set 'em loose! That Weather c'n have her huskies!"

Jenn started to do as she was bid, and together they set the leading team free, then the next. They did this all down the line until all the loads were standing free of the dogs.

"Mush!" Tommy shouted, clapping his hands. "Mush!"

All the dogs set off into the mist, leaving the loads of hailstones standing with their parrot drivers.

"Go on, you lot, hop off!" Tommy screeched at the birds, and they too vanished. Half flying, half hopping after the dogs.

"Now what?" Jenn cried, breathing hard from her exertions. "Ten loads o' hailstones wi' nowhere to go!"

"You reckon?" Tommy grinned. "Come on lass, push!"

Slowly the sledge started to move, then faster as it glided over the ice. On, and on until, "Let go, lass!" Tommy cried. He grabbed Jenn's hand and pulled her away from the moving load as it toppled over into the smoking vent.

From a safe distance they stood watching the sudden explosion of steam from the vent. It was a fearsome sight. The whole area around was smothered in steam for some minutes, and they had to move far back to escape it. Finally, it cleared away and Jenn looked at Tommy in awe.

"Tommy, you reckon that low loader will have done a lot o' damage? Smashin' down that chimney?"

"Won't do as much damage as them hailstones would – if that Weather had got hold of 'em to drop on Lancashire. Come on, lass, next load for the drop."

They set the next low loader moving, tipped it finally into the vent, and ran away from the steam which suddenly billowed up. Then, one by one, they toppled over the other loads into the smoking vent.

Finally the job was done, and they waited till the steam cleared away across the ice before venturing to the edge of the vent. The whole place down below seemed to be boiling like a volcano.

Jenn pulled away. "I'm scared, Tommy, scared!"

Tommy dropped down on the ice edge, peering over. Suddenly, something huge came rushing up at him, and he scrabbled back from the side with a cry of fear. "A shark!"

"I saw it Tommy, I saw it!" Jenn cried, running

away in her fright.

"Jenn! Wait lass, wait!" Tommy screamed after her. "You're heading for that smoke cloud!"

Jenn stopped and stood breathing heavily, waiting for Tommy to catch up. He came skating up to her at speed. "It's all right now! That shark can't touch us."

"A *shark*, Tommy, a shark, swimmin' in fog!"

"Aye, an' real enough. You know it snapped off a piece o' ice from t'side when it come up at us? I heard the crunch."

"What are we goin' to do now, Tommy?" asked Jenn.

"Go an' find Blackpool Tower, like I said. There's no other way to get down, lass."

They went off across the ice in the direction Blackpool Tower might be. Tommy was guessing, but they were due for a bit of luck sometime.

"How far've we gone you reckon?" Jenn said.

"Hundred miles, way my legs feel," Tommy muttered. "Come on, lass, we've gotta keep movin'. When we land at t'Tower somebody'll give us a meal."

They set off once more, still making good progress. Once they stopped to look back. The Tower at Rimington was just visible in the hazy distance.

"Wish I'd brought my camera," Tommy said with deep regret. "Jus' think what pictures we could take!"

"Look!" Jenn cried in alarm, pointing ahead

towards Blackpool. "More smoke belchin' out from a dozen places!"

"We'll move round it, lass, come on!"

They began to skate once more, steadily advancing on the spreading cloud of smoke until Tommy pulled Jenn to a stop. "Wait, lass, wait!"

"What's do, Tommy?"

"Must be some big town, Preston probably. All them factory chimneys in one area. We'll scout round it."

They moved southwards for several hundred yards, but suddenly Tommy stopped. "Don't move, lass, smoke's spreadin' – like – fog! An' get your hanky out to cover your mouth!"

"Lost it, Tommy, remember?"

"Use mine then!"

"What about you?"

"I'll – think o' somethin'. Here!"

Jenn took the handkerchief gratefully, and pushed it over her face just as the thick, black smoke came floating towards them. She was aware of Tommy pulling up his shirt from his pants, and putting it over his face.

Almost at once they were enveloped in the smoke. So much that they became invisible even to each other for a frightening moment.

"Jenn!" Tommy spluttered, and then, as she answered with his name, they held hands tightly.

"I know what it is!" Tommy said suddenly. "A cooling tower at some power station! Must be! Heat

melts the ice, like heat from smoke melts it in all them other vents!"

"Then – then there's *water* down there," Jenn whispered. "If only – if only we'd the nerve to dive in! We c'n both swim like fish! Let's dive in, Tommy!"

"Don't be daft! I'll bet there's sharks, an' all kinds o' monsters in there! Besides, this steam means hot water, we'd be scalded to death in a minute."

"I never thought o' that."

"Come on, lass," Tommy said, pulling at her

hand, "let's go before somethin' comes up, an' grabs us."

"Aye, Tommy," Jenn said sadly.

They were just about to move away from the edge of the steam crater when something did come up out of it! A flock of birds of all things.

"Look, Jenn!" Tommy cried in great excitement. "Jus' look at them!"

Jenn had seen them at the same moment, and together they stood there on the ice, just staring. The birds were large ones, and to Tommy, very familiar. As they flew overhead he pointed at them in dismay. "Vultures!"

"Vultures!" Jenn echoed in a frightened voice. "Are you sure, Tommy?"

"Jus' look at 'em!" Tommy told her. "Seen vultures many a time on t'telly; followin' folk in deserts. Waitin' for 'em to die so they c'n pick their bones!"

"Shut up, Tommy!"

"Jus' watch 'em hover!" Tommy cried, still excited by the mere sight of them as they wheeled, and hovered, in turn.

"Let's get away from here, Tommy, please! They scare me to death!"

"Aye. Come on. They'll maybe go back down this vent when we do. Vultures is from hot countries, that's why they hang out in this steam vent."

They began to skate off over the ice in the general direction of where they hoped Blackpool might be. When they stopped for a breather, and turned their eyes behind them the vultures had vanished.

"Thank goodness!" Jenn cried in great relief.

"Oh, no!" Tommy gasped. "Look, up there over our heads!"

Jenn looked, and gasped now with fear. The orange sky was scarred by the dark silhouettes of a dozen or so vultures, hovering right above them.

Tommy and Jenn quickly moved off once more, skating like mad. When they stopped for another breather they stared upwards. It was as if they'd never moved from last time they stopped. The vultures were following them, stalking them, waiting with bird patience for them to collapse, perhaps.

"Come on, lass!" Tommy cried urgently. "We've gotta find that tower quick, before them vultures swoop!"

They set off again across the ice, their eyes staring in all directions ahead. Aware, without having to look, that the vultures were keeping pace over their heads.

4

They must have been travelling for a good half hour without a rest. Finally Tommy pulled to a stop, and Jenn and he looked at each other, breathing hard for some time.

It was Tommy who looked up first, fully expecting the vultures to be wheeling about overhead.

"They've gone, lass, gone!" he cried, after scanning the sky.

"Thank heaven for that!" Jenn said with relief.

They rested a while, then set off once more. Tommy had used the sun for a marker; now and then looking over his shoulder as they'd skated towards the coast. So that he was pretty confident they were going roughly in the right direction.

After some minutes Tommy whooped out excitedly, and pointed dead ahead. "T'tower, lass! Stickin' up out o' t'ice!"

They set off feverishly for the landmark. They kept their eyes on it every second, and finally Tommy raced ahead. He could make out the tower quite

plainly now, and couldn't contain his eagerness.

Jenn pushed her tired legs harder, and chased after him. At last they were there, right beside what was definitely Blackpool Tower, the familiar painted structure they'd both seen with their parents last summer.

Tommy could remember so vividly leaning over the side of the main viewing platform on all four sides, and trying to see better through the iron safety railings. Staring in wonder at the whole of

Lancashire laid out before his feasting eyes, with the blue sea swelling out on the other side.

Now the main platform was below the ice, set solid in it. Only the upper, smaller, platform with its narrow iron steps was visible.

Tommy climbed up on to the structure, and rattled the railings with a piece of wood he found in a corner.

"Help!" he shouted at the top of his voice. "Help! Somebody, help!"

Jenn climbed over to join him, and they shouted together. Nobody answered, nothing happened.

"There's nobody there!" Jenn cried. "Nobody there at all! We'll never get out, Tommy!"

"Winter season," Tommy muttered angrily. "I bet they've closed up for t'winter season."

"There should be folk here, for them Illuminations!"

"Illuminations are over wi'," Tommy cried. "There'll be nobody here till next summer."

"We can't stop here till next summer!"

"I know that, lass!" Tommy scouted round the platform for something to prise at the solid ice with. There was nothing. A few seagulls – cut from books obviously, because there was writing on some of them – were flying round, and landing on the tip of the tower.

"I wonder," Tommy cried, "if we could stick it out here – till t'fog goes!"

"That Weather says it'll be foggy—" Jenn began, and Tommy finished it for her excitedly–"all day, an' half the night! It's not so long, lass, we c'n stick it out. Then, when t'fog's gone there's nothin' to stop us runnin' down them steps, an' ringin' that lift bell. Somebody'll be around, caretakers, tower minders, *somebody!*"

"Aye, Tommy – " Jenn cried – "*if* the ice melts. It's not ordinary fog this, it's – magic fog. It's magic, like nobody ever see except us."

"Aye, lass," Tommy whispered, putting his arm round her shoulder.

Then suddenly the magic was gone. The seagulls screamed in a flutter of fear, and winged their way off towards where the Irish Sea must be.

"What's up wi' them?" Tommy cried, staring upwards. Then he knew. A flock of birds came wheeling down from the orange sky, screeching loudly. One moment they were dark silhouettes against the sky, the next they were fluttering round their heads, trying to peck at their faces!

The vultures were back!

Tommy and Jenn threw up their hands, and tried to fight them off, but it was no use. The vultures kept coming in like war planes, seeming to dive bomb them without actually hitting them with anything except these final pecks.

It was enough. After some seconds the two frightened children had to leave their position on top of Blackpool Tower. They clambered down on to the ice, and ran.

After some fifty yards they both stopped, looking

back in fear that the vultures would follow up their attack.

To their great relief they merely perched on the top of the tower, staring across the ice at them.

"I – I thought they were go'nna rip us to bits!" Jenn cried in a shaky voice. "Thought we were done for that time!"

"We are done for, lass," Tommy said in a flat voice. "They've driven us off t'tower!"

"They'll go, sometime," Jenn said, none too confidently.

"They won't, lass, don't you see? That Weather woman, she controls everythin' up here. She had them wolves doin' her work back at Rimington; like sheepdogs, roundin' us up till she could talk to us."

Jenn's eyes were wide with dismay now.

"Then – we can't wait until this fog melts away! We can't get back on to Blackpool Tower!"

"No chance, lass. We – gotta go back to Rimington, back to her."

"Tommy, we'll never get down then! Let's try them vultures, eh? Try to see if we c'n – shoo 'em off that Tower!"

"Waste o' time."

"Let's *try*, Tommy!"

"OK. We'll try."

They walked slowly back to the tower. Four yards away they stopped, staring up at the vultures. This was the first time they'd actually been close enough – apart from trying furiously to drive them away – to study them. They were horrible, like feathered ghouls perched on gravestones in a cemetery.

Tommy and Jenn waved their arms, shouted, hooted, threatened. They might not have been there for all the notice the birds took of them.

"Come on, lass," Tommy said in final despair, "that Weather works 'em like robots! They've been told to get us off that tower, an' keep us off."

Jenn wouldn't be convinced. With a sudden whoop of anger she ran at the Tower framework, her arms like whirling windmills.

The vultures rose into the air, and came at her with loud screeches.

Jenn fled across the ice, past Tommy who could only stand for a moment, paralysed. Then he too set off after Jenn, and only when they were completely out of breath did they finally stop.

When they looked around into the sky there were no vultures.

"Jenn, I told you!" Tommy cried in deep reproof. "I told you they were only keepin' us off t'tower!"

"Let's go back then," Jenn murmured, heavily depressed now. "I only hope that Weather don't try her experiments on me!"

They started to walk across the ice, then skate. Now and then they passed vents with wisps of smoke coming up them. One such place even had the shape of a chimney quite visible several feet down, its brickwork blackened by the smoke of years.

"If only we dared drop down on to that brickwork!" Tommy cried. "I bet there's even a – a ladder goin' down to t'ground! We could be home in another hour."

"Home," Jenn whispered unhappily, "we'll never see home again."

Tommy teetered on the edge of the vent, judging the distance. "I've half a mind to risk a jump!"

Jenn pulled him back hastily. "Don't, Tommy, don't! Look at that fog swirlin' around t'top o' the chimney, heaven knows what sort o' monster is lurkin' in it, waitin' for us to try to escape!"

"You're right, lass," Tommy said regretfully. "Come on, let's get back to Rimington. At least we're on familiar ground there."

They started off once more, and suddenly, after

another half hour's skating, they saw some sort of a barrier, like a high fence, going away in both directions. It barred their path to the top of Rimington.

"What is it, Tommy?" Jenn cried.

"Let's find out!"

Tommy set off at a fair speed, with Jenn close up behind him. As they came within a few yards they could see the vivid colouring.

"What is it?" Jenn said, staring in wonder at the fence-like apparition. Six feet high it was, roughly, and the colouring, in strips, was marvellous. Simply marvellous.

"Jenn!" Tommy gasped out finally. "I know what it is! It's a rainbow! Look, all the colours are right! Red, orange, yellow, green, blue, ind—indigo, an' – an' violet. It's a rainbow!"

"A rainbow?" Jenn laughed. "Don't be daft, Tommy, rainbows are in t' *sky*, not stacked out like a fence!"

"It *is* a rainbow, must be!"

"It's straight, rainbows are curved, like an arch!"

Tommy put his hand out carefully towards the vivid colours.

"What're you doin'?" Jenn said quickly.

"Seein' what it's made of."

"Might be electrified!"

"Electrified!" Tommy laughed, and pushed his hand into the coloured fence boldly. Even so he was quivering with a kind of fear. He could feel something, yet not feel something. Like putting his hand into driven snow.

"I didn't turn to a cinder, anyway!" he laughed. "It's – funny."

"Funny, is it?" a voice came at them from across the other side of the rainbow. "I suppose that was funny too, running my whole stock of hailstones into the vents!" The Weather was hovering at the end of the rainbow, her pages fluttering angrily.

"How do you know that?" Jenn cried.

"I heard the whole wicked tale from the parrots. But you'll pay for that adventure, never fear!"

"What do you want?" Tommy demanded. "An'

what do you mean setting sharks, an' vultures on us?"

"I set nothing on nobody, boy! I may *suggest*, but creatures of fur and feather merely follow their particular instincts."

"You threatened us wi' wolves when we were here before!" Jenn put in sharply.

"Did I now? I merely flicked a page at them, I never *asked* them to attack you, did I? I told you, they follow their own instincts."

"I've a good mind," Tommy said, pushing through the rainbow towards her, "to rip out a few o' your pages!"

"Have you now?" the Weather chuckled. "Try it, boy, if you must."

"Don't, Tommy!" Jenn cried, grabbing hold of his arm.

"Let him, if he finds pleasure in it! Go on, boy, rip! But be warned, the more pages you rip out the less weather there'll be for me to bother about!"

"What do you mean?" Tommy said, pulled up in his tracks.

"Obvious, surely!" the Weather whirred briskly. "Each page is for one day of the year. No page for any one day, no weather!"

"There must be *some* sort o' weather!" Jenn argued.

The Weather flicked through a few pages, and a chuckle escaped her.

"Try August Bank Holiday for instance. I'm down

for sunshine all day – I was in a generous mood when I filled that in. Rip that out, and what do we get? No sun, no *anything*."

"There's got to be something," Tommy argued, "clouds, at least. You can't have a day wi' no weather!"

"No weather means no weather!" the book snapped. "No sun, no clouds, no blue sky, no breeze. Just a – blank."

"A blank?" Jenn queried.

"People will get up, and they'll expect the sun to rise at such and such a time. It won't. The darkness will persist all day. Like a television screen when you switch off."

"Poppycock!" Tommy cried. "Where did you see a television screen up here? How do you know what it looks like?"

"My magazines, of course. You forget, I've been here since time began."

"I believe her," Jenn said slowly. "Don't try anythin', Tommy, or we could mess up the whole summer!"

"Try ripping out a few pages for January if you must, boy," the Weather coaxed him slyly. "I've a freeze-up set for the third. Lasting two days. Go on, remove a week or two!"

"What'd happen then?" Jenn asked uneasily.

"The whole country would be a solid block of ice until we got back to normal. Of course, by then, there'd be no people left for me to bother about. All

frozen stiff in their ice blocks."

"You're mad!" Tommy cried angrily.

"Mad? I am, boy, at this very minute! Mad at you two for wasting half a day at the seaside. Come on now, to work at once!"

"Work?" Jenn asked her, puzzled. "What sort o' work?"

"You can start on this rainbow for instance. I've a sudden thunderstorm to do in two days' time. I need a rainbow to finish off with. People like rainbows after a storm, and I'm feeling in a good mood of a sudden."

"What," Tommy said flatly, "can we do wi' a rainbow?"

"Bend it, boy, bend it! Can't you see that it's quite straight? Did you ever see a straight rainbow in the sky?"

"Never," Jenn admitted.

"Nor me," Tommy said thoughtfully.

"Right then, bend it." The Weather flicked a page at the rainbow. "It was made a half hour back, it's ready to set at any moment. As soon as you can feel it you can start bending it."

"Where?" Tommy said, touching the rainbow, and feeling that it really had gone stiff, like a man's collar.

"Where?" The Weather pointed a page at the hill on which Rimington Pike's tower stood sentinel. "Round the hill of course! You, girl, take this end; you, boy, run to the other. It's quite a distance, so hurry. When you reach rainbow's end take a firm hold, and move inwards. The girl will do the same at this end. Keep going into the side of the hill till you can go no further. When you feel the rainbow tugging you'll know it's finished, bent round the base of the hill. A perfect arc."

"So that's how they make rainbows!" Tommy said in deep admiration.

"That's how we bend them," the Weather replied. "Making them is much more difficult. I've donkeys

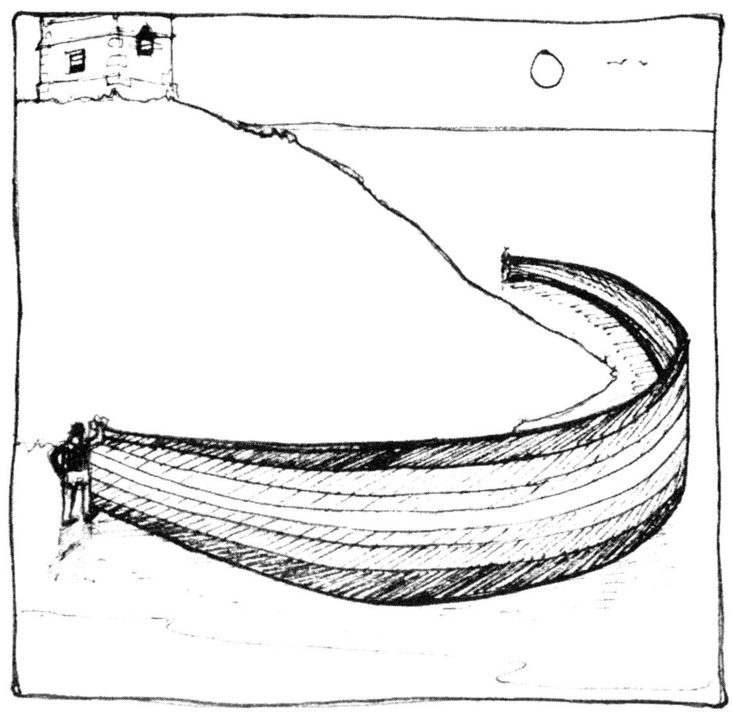

on that task at the moment, and you know how silly donkeys are. I've had rejects, colours in the wrong place, things like that. Once I had to put out a *tartan* rainbow because I'd a Scottish terrier on the job. Strange you didn't notice down there."

"Could you do Manchester United colours?" Tommy cried excitedly.

"To work, boy!" the Weather cried angrily.

To work they went, Tommy skating along the length of the rainbow till he reached the far end. When he reached there he waved to Jenn, a mere doll-size figure now.

Together they grasped the rainbow, and together, although so far apart, they moved inwards. After a while Tommy felt the pressure of the hill, and he kept on pushing until he could do no more.

"Right!" the Weather boomed out. "Pull it free, stack it over there behind the cloud corrals!"

"The – cloud corrals?" Tommy said, gaping at her.

"Cloud corrals," the Weather flicked at him impatiently, "are no different from the corrals used on ranches for horses, boy. Where do you reckon clouds go when there's a clear sky?"

"Never thought," Tommy admitted.

"Where do you think clear skies go when there are clouds?"

"They don't *go* anywhere!" Jenn laughed, having run up to them excitedly. "Clear skies are behind the clouds of course!"

"That's what you think, girl! We take them in for cleaning. Blue skies, grey skies, red-skies-at-night. You never wondered how they keep their colours so well? Because we have them cleaned regularly up here!"

"I suppose," Tommy said slyly, "you polish t'rain as well! Drop by drop!"

"We do, we have to. Boy, how do you people manage to get my rain so filthy, eh? You really should be more careful, you know. After all it's not given, only lent. Things lent should be returned in the same condition they were received!"

"I'll remember that, next time I get soaked to me skin!" Tommy cried cheekily.

Suddenly it started to rain! Right in front of them, but leaving the ice at their feet untouched. The two children gaped at this fresh wonder.

"Go on, take that rainbow, and stack it with the others!" the Weather cut at them impatiently.

"We'll get wet through!" Tommy cried, pulling back from the rain.

"Pull it on one side, silly boy!"

"Pull it – on one – side?"

"Like this!" The Weather floated over to where the

rain was now fairly belting down. She flicked a page at them, and a kind of titter came out of her covers.

"Silly boy, it's not *raining!* This is the cleaning drop. A continuous belt of rain going round on a spinning drum way up in the sky. Too far up for you to see it. It passes each drop through a fluffy cloud five times. Then the rain stops till we can change it for the next thousand gallons."

"You stack the rain in oil drums then?" Tommy said, still in a sly mood despite the wonders he'd seen.

"We stack it in rain clouds, of course, boy! See them way up yonder? Where else? Come on now, I want that rainbow stacked away, there'll be another coming along shortly to be bent. Hurry!"

"We'll get wet through I told you!" Tommy protested.

"Pull it on one side, like a curtain!"

"It's *rain!*" Tommy protested. "Not beads on strings!"

"You don't believe, even now, that things aren't the same up here as they are down below? Pull it on one side, girl, show him!"

"Me?" Jenn said. "But—"

"Imagine it's a curtain, girl, and it will be a curtain!"

Jenn looked at the rain as it came splashing down on the cold ice before her. She pulled her lips tight, and stepped forward, her hand outstretched as if actually pulling open the window curtains at home. Suddenly the rain parted to her touch, and she went through in complete safety.

As Tommy just gaped Jenn shouted at him: "Fantastic, Tommy, fantastic! A curtain of rain. I'll never get wet again – when I get back home, never!"

"Get that rainbow stacked, and quickly!" the Weather cried impatiently. "And hurry back for the next one. See, it's being brought out by the Scottish Terriers already. If it isn't made into an arc within fifteen minutes it'll break in bits. They're brittle, you know. Hurry!"

They grabbed the rainbow, Jenn in front. With one hand she pulled open the rain, moved through with the rainbow gliding smoothly on the ice.

Way at the other end Tommy followed her. When he too reached the rain drop he tugged at it with a firm hand. The rain didn't turn into a curtain for him. By the time he'd got through the water he was soaking wet.

"I'm not standing this!" Tommy bellowed angrily, squeezing water from his clothes. "Jenn, we're goin' home!"

"How?" Jenn shouted back from the other end of the rainbow.

"How? I don't know, but we're goin'!"

5

Tommy and Jenn worked hard on the rainbows, with the Weather hovering about menacingly every time they stopped for a rest. She seemed to have no pity, no feelings for humans at all.

"What about some food?" Tommy said after they'd done five rainbows.

"Food?" the Weather flicked at them impatiently. "I forgot humans need food! A pity you're not cut-outs; they don't need food!"

"I wondered how all these birds and animals managed wi'out food!" Tommy said, interested in that problem. "An' why do you make so many?"

"I have to experiment, don't I? Ninety-nine times out of a hundred my cut-outs are useless for the jobs I need doing. *Hands*, that's what I need, *hands!*" She crinkled her pages, hovering round them, especially interested in Jenn.

Jenn was scared by the way she acted, and backed away.

"The cloud corral is my main worry," the Weather

went on with a resentful whirl of her pages. "Clouds arriving in their scores sometimes, and nobody to clean them properly for the next batch I have to send out. Storm clouds are no problem, they fill automatically, and are naturally dirty. It's the pretty fluffs, and puffs, and the odd woollies, which are hardest. I have rabbits using other rabbits as dusters on them. It isn't really practical, and it's so *slow*. Rabbits *will* play about."

"What about some food?" Tommy cut in on her moanings.

"Oh, if you must eat, I suppose you must. I've got to keep your strength up, you've hard work ahead. Forever. Unless—"

"Unless what?" Jenn said, feeling frightened again.

"Never mind. Go to that hut there, it's my office. A cut-out from some handyman magazine. There are a few other books in a corner, among them one for cooking food. Useless rubbish."

"We can't eat *paper!*" Tommy cried angrily.

"Did I ask you to, boy?"

Inside, the hut was a bare room with just one table and one stool.

The books were stacked in a corner, and one was a recipe book. Jenn and Tommy went through it carefully, uselessly.

"Makes me feel more hungry!" Tommy cried, skimming it back in the corner.

The Weather came in behind them as he did so. "Hurry up with your dinner!"

"We're *not* eatin' paper!" Jenn cried, as angry as Tommy now.

"Cut it out, you sillies!"

Tommy stared at the Weather in sudden understanding. "You mean – it'll turn into food, real food, if we do?"

"Everything which is cut out up here turns into the real thing. Everything, that is, except people. People are stupid."

"What do we use?" Jenn asked her, mildly excited now. "There aren't any scissors."

"Use your two fingers, clip-clip! Did you never use them as a child? Playing at cut-outs?"

"Course I did!" Jenn cried. "You mean—"

"Try it, and don't waste any more time!"

In spite of everything that had happened, Jenn had doubts. She made a pair of scissors with her two fingers, flicked them once or twice to get used to the idea. Then took a page with dumplings, and stewed

steak, and lots of gravy on a large plate. She began her cutting action, right up to the paper. To her complete surprise, and Tommy's utter disbelief, her fingers cut neatly through the paper. The second she had cut it away, click, it was *real*.

Jenn held it in her hands, steaming now, smelling wonderful.

"Hoo! It's too hot to hold!"

"Put it on the table then, silly!" the Weather crinkled.

Jenn laid it down carefully, and stood there, just staring down at it, her head shaking slowly from side to side.

"I'll have a go at that!" Tommy cried, his eyes wide with excitement, and hunger.

He tried, and failed, tried again, and failed again. He was about to give up when Jenn, ever gentle, touched his fingers with her own. "Tommy, even ordinary scissors won't work if you grab them like – like a pair of garden shears! Easy, Tommy, gently."

"Eh?" Tommy looked at her, looked at the meal she'd fashioned from paper. Then he nodded, set his jaw, and cut the paper as if his hands were feathers. It worked! *Click*. Fish and chips, and mushy peas!

They'd no cutlery, but Tommy thumbed through a mail-order book, and found a box of knives, forks, and spoons. Inside a minute Jenn had cut them out, and they were *real*. They set to with their dinner, and both felt they'd never had a finer meal. Tea was served from a china teapot Jenn picked out. The tea, milk, and sugar were found in another cookery book.

"Finished!" the Weather flicked at them suddenly.

"Not quite," Tommy spluttered through a mouthful of jam roll, and custard.

"Finished!" the Weather cut at him like a whiplash. "Not a question, a statement of fact! You can go to the skies now, set to cleaning them!"

Tommy swallowed the last of his sweet, then gulped.

"What skies?"

"Phizz! The stupidity of the boy! Haven't I explained fully that we have lots of skies? In all colours? What about all those wonderful summer sunsets, and fine sunrises I give you every year? I've only so many, boy! Each one is stacked neatly beside the other, in mothballs till they're needed. Plus a variety of moons to match different colours. Full moon, new moon, half moon."

"There's only *one* moon!" Tommy spluttered in laughter.

"Is there now! Get off to those skies, you'll need to climb a ladder to reach them. Take a few rabbits with you, to use for dusting the skies. Don't forget, either, grey rabbits for the grey skies, black ones for stormy backgrounds, and night skies. Never use a grey rabbit to dust a blue sky, the colour goes smudgy, all mixed up."

They went and came suddenly on a line of moons, set up neatly like so many huge pictures on an ice rink. Vast they were; new moons – shining brilliantly, half moons, quarters.

"She was right, Tommy!" Jenn cried excitedly. "There *are* different moons for each night!"

"Never mind the moons!" Tommy said. "Let's get them skies cleaned, or she'll be after us again!"

"I thought we were gonna escape?" Jenn said, coming back to earth with a bump.

"I'll think o' somethin', lass, never fear."

"But she keeps lookin' at me, funny like!" Jenn muttered as they came upon a ladder going right up into the orange sky.

"I'll think o' somethin'! Come on, this ladder must be where we go."

"It goes a long way up, an' I'm scared o' heights!" Jenn said fearfully.

"I'll follow you up, lass, you'll be OK."

They climbed the ladder for quite some way, then suddenly it finished as a wide platform. For a moment or two they stood on this in new wonder, just staring.

Skies there were in all colours, lying about like so many massive tablecloths under the light of the brass sun way above. They would have to walk on them to clean them. Jenn began to take off her clogs.

"What're you doin' that for?" Tommy asked her.

"You'd best do it too, Tommy, she'll go mad if we mark these skies with our clogs!"

Tommy took off his clogs resentfully, then snapped his fingers in irritation.

"What's do now?" Jenn asked him.

"We've come up wi'out dusters!"

"You mean – rabbits!"

"Dusters, rabbits, we've come wi'out any!"

Jenn stared past him, and pointed. "Look, a big box over by the side o' the platform. I wonder—"

They hurried over to the box. It was full to the brim with rabbits of all colours, neatly stacked together, munching contentedly on greens.

They took a supply over to the skies. The rabbits didn't seem to mind, they must have gone through this routine many a time.

"I wonder who dusted before we came?" Jenn said thoughtfully. "Difficult wi' no hands." She was busy dusting the very black sky, holding the rabbit carefully so as not to hurt it, moving from one side to the other neatly.

"That's why she needs people, lass." Tommy stood up a minute, holding his aching back. "Hands aren't plentiful apart from people."

"Monkeys have hands," Jenn said.

"Gorillas," Tommy put in. "I've never seen any."

The Weather was hovering again, right in front of them.

"Shirking again!" she whirred angrily.

"It's hard work, bending down like this!" Tommy shot back at her. "What about a tea break?"

"A tea break!" the Weather cut through her pages sharply.

"No tea break, no work!" Tommy persisted. "We're on strike!"

"Nobody goes on *strike* up here!"

"Everybody goes on strike, down there!" Tommy said firmly.

"A tea break," the Weather seemed to be browsing through her pages with thought. "Right, you shall have it. One half-hour, no more!"

They put back their dusters, and hurried to put on their clogs. Then it was clatter-clatter on the ladder.

They made some tea in the china teapot. Tommy swallowed his in one gulp, and then ran over to the corner where the magazines were.

"Watch the door, lass!" he cried, and quickly thumbed through the books. He took one and pushed it inside his trousers so there'd be no bulge.

"What're you doin', Tommy?" Jenn asked him, sipping the last of her tea.

"Never you mind, lass! Be ready for anythin', anythin'! I didn't like the way that Weather give in to us about a tea break. She's up to somethin'!"

"What am I up to, boy?" the Weather was back

once more.

"Nothin'," Tommy said innocently. "Nothin'."

"Now, girl," she went on crisply, "you've had your tea break. Work!"

"We've only had ten minutes!" Tommy protested.

"Work!"

"Why ain't there any monkeys?" Tommy asked. "You say you need hands. They've got hands."

"What a clever boy you are!" the Weather flicked at him. "I've got monkeys, I've got gorillas. Who do you think does my cutting out, eh? Up in the tower? That's my production room. Those other wolves which chased you off the tower a while back; just cut out that very minute. Be warned again, boy! For some reason I can't get them to do the work of people. They're vicious! So don't go near them if you value your lives."

"You said it won't work wi' people, cuttin' out," Jenn cried in a burst of defiance. "I'm glad!"

"Glad, are you, girl? Get me that magazine on its own by the door. Quickly!"

Jenn saw the solitary book, and brought it over, laying it on the table.

"Now, girl, cut!"

"Cut what?" Jenn said, acting stupid for no reason.

"This book of course! Fool I've been, since you came into my kingdom. Not to realise the truth! The days, and weeks I've wasted, trying to get my monkeys, and gorillas to cut out people. It never

worked, of course. I can make sharks swim in fog, and vultures nest in steam cooling towers, but people are so stubborn! The Weather moved right up to Jenn, her pages fairly humming. "Cut, girl, cut! I know now that all it needs to cut out people is *people!* So, cut!"

"You can't make slaves of people like that!" Jenn cried in horror. "People should be free!"

"People?" the Weather whirred. "Look at this magazine, girl, a children's fashion book. Far better to control than grown-ups, children! Cut! I want an army of children to work my clouds, and my rainbows, and my peals of thunder. Cut, or you'll go to the wind tunnels as I promised you earlier!"

The Weather paused a moment, then a heavy chuckle came from her pages. "You won't like my wind tunnels. I test the speed of high winds, and hurricanes and blizzards in there, you know, by the time it takes for an object to be blown one mile. I use balloons now, but I can just as easily use *girls* – and *boys*!"

"You wouldn't do that with us!" Jenn cried in alarm. "You couldn't be so cruel!"

"Cut!" the Weather flicked flatly.

"Jenn!" Tommy cried, grabbing her arm. "This is it! We've gotta run, now! Run, or she'll have us here all our lives!"

Jenn skimmed the fashion magazine away, and ran to the door with Tommy. They didn't turn to look back, but raced off across the ice towards the foot of the hill on which the tower stood.

Behind them the Weather was whirring frantically, like a mass of paper trapped on fencing in a fierce gale.

"Where to?" Jenn cried, breathless already.

"Tower!" Tommy cried.

"Tower?" Jenn cried in alarm. "There's vicious gorillas, an' monkeys in there!"

"There'll be wolves after us in a minute, lass! I need time to make somethin'! Run, up that hill!"

Tommy almost pushed Jenn up the last few yards, and when they looked back they could see a pack of wolves massing at the bottom.

"Why don't they come, an' get it over with?" Jenn

cried in deep despair.

"That Weather thinks she's got us, lass. She's got them wolves hangin' about below, knowin' we have to go back if we want to get away from here."

"We'll never get away, never!" Jenn cried. "Let's give in!"

"An' cut out other kids to work themselves to the bone?"

"What *can* we do then?"

"This!" Tommy said, pulling open the magazine

he'd carried in his hand all the way up the hill. He quickly thumbed through the pages, and then turned the book inside out.

"Look, lass, a spade. Watch!" Tommy began to use his fingers for scissors, and the spade suddenly became real. Then he did the same with a pick. Putting these on the ground Tommy quickly thumbed through the book again.

"Ah!"

He used his scissors once more on a new page. A

suit of armour rattled to the ground, then another, slightly smaller! Jenn could only stare at this new miracle.

"Jus' what we need, lass!" Tommy cried excitedly. "This is a story book of knights, and people like that. I've cut the tools from an advert. I hope these suits of armour aren't too big. Get in one, quick!"

It took some time, but finally Tommy had got Jenn into hers. Then he managed to climb into the other just as a gorilla popped its head over the top of the tower above them. The gorilla growled loudly, glared at them, then vanished in fear at the unusual sight!

"Come on, lass," Tommy cried, "I'll take the tools. Mind you don't slip on this hill, or them wolves'll be on you!"

"Thanks for cheerin' me up!" Jenn cried, her voice muffled inside the visor. Yet she went down the hill slowly, very carefully, with Tommy following closely behind.

Near to the bottom the wolves came at them, yapping and howling round their legs helplessly. Even in the excitement and danger of the moment Tommy couldn't help wondering about how they must look. Two kids in knights' armour, and wearing clogs!

Right at the edge of the ice Tommy gave Jenn the spade.

"Keep these wolves off me wi' that," he cried over the sound of the howling, "while I dig down!"

The Weather appeared as Tommy started to dig into the ground at the edge of the ice. Fluttering her pages about in a frenzy of anger.

"Worry them! Worry them like sheep!" she commanded, but the wolves could do nothing against armour and a whirling spade!

Now and then Tommy changed over to the spade, gradually digging down into the soil. Finally a hole appeared, and wisps of fog came seeping up.

Tommy attacked the hole with greater frenzy, sweating madly now in his armour. Then he stood up, his head towards Jenn. "Go on, lass, down into the hole! I'll keep these wolves off!"

He whirled the spade in one hand, the pick in the other, as Jenn dropped down, and somehow wriggled through out of sight.

It was a near thing with Tommy. He had to let go of the tools as he too dropped down into the hole he'd made beneath the thick ice. The whole pack seemed to crowd in on him, almost falling into the hole with him.

Then, suddenly, he was through! Clear! With Jenn standing before him with her face all red from her own exertions.

Jenn, wearing only her own clothes. With no sign of the armour she'd come down through the hole in.

"Tommy! Your armour's vanished!" Jenn cried.

He looked down at himself, and nodded in new disbelief. Like Jenn he was dressed normally!

"Magic!" Tommy said, staring upwards into the fog. "There's nothin' there any more, except fog, nothin'!"

They went slowly back down the path homewards to Arpull. They stopped once or twice to look back, but there was nothing except fog.

"Do you think we – dreamed it, Tommy?" Jenn said.

Tommy shook his head, his eyes bright with wonder.

"No, lass, we didn't dream any of it. There's another world up there, where they make the weather. Maybe, one day, we'll go back."

"Aye, one day," Jenn whispered.

They went on down the hill.